Follow the Way of Love

A PASTORAL MESSAGE TO FAMILIES

UNITED STATES CONFERENCE OF CATHOLIC BISHOPS
WASHINGTON, D.C.

Follow the Way of Love: A Pastoral Message of the U.S. Catholic Bishops to Families was developed by the Committee on Marriage and Family. It was approved by the Administrative Committee in September 1993 and by the Catholic bishops of the United States at their general meeting on November 17, 1993. *Follow the Way of Love* is authorized by the undersigned.

Monsignor Robert N. Lynch
General Secretary
NCCB/USCC

In 2001 the National Conference of Catholic Bishops/United States Catholic Conference became the United States Conference of Catholic Bishops.

This message was delivered on the occasion of the United Nations 1994 International Year of the Family.

Photos credits: Family Time, Volume 124, Corbis Images; Family Living, Digital Stock.

Scriptural excerpts from the *New American Bible* used with permission of the copyright holder, Confraternity of Christian Doctrine, copyright ©1970, 1986. All rights reserved.

First Printing, January 1994
Tenth Printing, October 2002

Contents

The family exists

at the heart of all societies.

It is the first and

most basic community to

which every person belongs.

There is nothing

more fundamental to

our vitality as a society

and as a Church.

Foreword

T he family exists at the heart of all societies. It is the first and most basic community to which every person belongs. There is nothing more fundamental to our vitality as a society and as a Church. For, in the words of Pope John Paul II, "The future of humanity passes by way of the family" (*On the Family*, no. 86).

Thus, it is fitting that the United Nations has drawn attention to the condition of family life throughout the world. By designating 1994 the International Year of the Family, it has invited everyone—especially families—to deepen their understanding of family life, to identify matters important to the family's well-being, and to take action that will strengthen families.

This message of the United States Catholic bishops to families takes as a starting point the International Year and its theme, *Family: Resources and*

Responsibilities in a Changing World. It invites families to examine the quality of their lives. It asks them to reflect on their strengths as well as their weaknesses; on their resources as well as their needs.

The message shares with families a vision of their great calling that is rooted in Christ's teaching and developed in the life of his believing community. It urges families to seek the healing, strength, and meaning that Christ offers through his Church. It pledges the support of the Church so that families might recognize their resources and carry out their responsibilities in a changing world.

This message stands within the tradition of teaching on marriage and family expressed through our Holy Father, the Second Vatican Council, and the National Conference of Catholic Bishops. Of necessity, it deals with only a few of the issues relevant to family life today. It offers a limited pastoral treatment of them consistent with the vocation of every Christian to *follow the way of love, even as Christ loved you* (cf. Eph 5:2).

The message is addressed primarily to Christian families but is intended also for all who can use it toward strengthening their families.

Questions are placed at various points in the message to encourage readers to make personal applications, as well as to use the text as the basis for discussion in their homes and with other families.

At the end of the message there is a select annotated list of church teaching on marriage and family.

Pastors and church ministers are encouraged to help families receive this message and use it.

Families Are a Sign of God's Presence

WAYS OF LOVING

When people talk about life in a family, they speak of love with its abiding peace, its searing pain, its moments of joy and disappointment, its heroic struggle and ordinary routines.

"Family is where someone loves you no matter what," a teenager declares.
*"Family doesn't mean just mom, dad, and kids, but grandparents,
aunts, uncles, and others,"* explains a Hispanic woman.
*"In a family you don't have to look very far to
find your cross,"* a father observes.
"My child asks me such mystical questions," reports a young
mother. *"I learn so much."*
*"My teenagers were very sensitive to me during my divorce.
God was there for me,"* a single parent recalls.

The story of family life is a story about love—shared, nurtured, and sometimes rejected or lost. In every family God is revealed uniquely and personally, for God is love and those who live in love, live in God and God dwells in them (cf. 1 Jn 4:16).

And so our message is one that springs from love and that offers you a reflection on love: how it is experienced in a family, how it is challenged today, how it grows and enriches others, and how it needs the support of the whole Church.

We write to you as pastors and teachers in the Church, but we come to you as family members also. We are sons and brothers and uncles. We have known the commitment and sacrifices of a mother and father, the warmth of a family's care, the happiness and pain that are part of loving.

Some of us lived in single-parent families; others were adopted children. Some of us grew up in alcoholic homes. We came from affluence and from families where money was scarce.

Some of us have felt the hurt of racial discrimination or cultural prejudice. Some have lived for many generations in this country. Others are recent immigrants.

With our families, we celebrate the birth of a baby or a loved one's success. We rejoice at weddings and anniversaries of family members even as we grieve at an untimely death or the breakup of a married couple.

Knowing your many joys and struggles, we value your witness of fidelity in marriage and in family life. We rejoice with you in your happiness. We walk with you in your sorrow.

THE WAY OF LOVE

Our ministry as pastors and teachers is enriched by our family experience. In addition, our vocation of leadership connects us to all families. It gives us the responsibility of opening up God's truth about human existence and of sharing with you the saving resources which the Lord has entrusted to the Church.

With our Holy Father, we consider it a privilege to undertake "the mission of proclaiming with joy and conviction the good news about the family" (*On the Family*, no. 86).

Yes, there is good news to tell. You may occasionally catch a glimpse of it in the news media and in conversation with neighbors or fellow workers. But the full story is to be found in God's word. The First Letter of John puts it succinctly:

> In this way the love of God was revealed to us: God sent his only Son into the world that we might have life through him. In this is love: not that we have loved God, but that he loved us. . . . Beloved, if God so loved us, we also must love one another. (1 Jn 4:9-11)

Thus, the basic vocation of every person, whether married or living a celibate life, is the same: *follow the way of love, even as Christ loved you* (cf. Eph 5:2). The Lord issues this call to your family and to every family regardless of its condition or circumstances.

Love brought you to life as a family. Love sustains you through good and bad times. When our Church teaches that the family is an "intimate community of life and love," it identifies something perhaps you already know and offers you a vision toward which to grow.

What you do in your family to create a community of love, to help each other to grow, and to serve those in need is critical, not only for your own sanctification but for the strength of society and our Church. It is a participation in the work of the Lord, a sharing in the mission of the Church. It is holy.

Reflection Questions

> 1. What image, feeling, or memory comes to mind when you think about your family?
> 2. What does it tell you about your life as a family?

YOU ARE THE CHURCH IN YOUR HOME

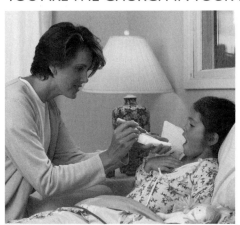

Baptism brings all Christians into union with God. Your family life is sacred because family relationships confirm and deepen this union and allow the Lord to work through you. The profound and the ordinary moments of daily life—mealtimes, workdays, vacations, expressions of love and intimacy, household chores, caring for a sick child or elderly parent, and even conflicts over things like how to celebrate holidays, discipline children, or spend money—all are the threads from which you can weave a pattern of holiness.

Jesus promised to be where two or three are gathered in his name (cf. Mt 18:20). We give the name *church* to the people whom the Lord gathers, who strive to follow his way of love, and through whose lives his saving presence is made known.

A family is our first community and the most basic way in which the Lord gathers us, forms us, and acts in the world. The early Church expressed this truth by calling the Christian family *a domestic church or church of the home.*

This marvelous teaching was underemphasized for centuries but reintroduced by the Second Vatican Council. Today we are still uncovering its rich treasure.

The point of the teaching is simple, yet profound. As Christian families, you not only belong to the Church, but your daily life is a true expression of the Church.

Your domestic church is not complete by itself, of course. It should be united with and supported by parishes and other communities within the larger Church. Christ has called you and joined you to himself in and through the sacraments. Therefore, you share in one and the same mission that he gives to the whole Church.

You carry out the mission of the church of the home in ordinary ways when:

- You **believe** in God and that God cares about you. It is God to whom you turn in times of trouble. It is God to whom you give thanks when all goes well.

- You **love** and never give up believing in the value of another person. Before young ones hear the Word of God preached from the pulpit, they form a picture of God drawn from their earliest experiences of being loved by parents, grandparents, godparents, and other family members.

- You **foster intimacy**, beginning with the physical and spiritual union of the spouses and extending in appropriate ways to the whole family. To be able to share yourself—good and bad qualities—within a family and to be accepted there is indispensable to forming a close relationship with the Lord.

- You **evangelize** by professing faith in God, acting in accord with gospel values, and setting an example of Christian living for your children and for others. And your children, by their spontaneous and genuine spirituality, will often surprise you into recognizing God's presence.

- You **educate**. As the primary teachers of your children, you impart knowledge of the faith and help them to acquire values necessary for Christian living. Your example is the most effective way to teach. Sometimes they listen and learn; sometimes they teach you new ways of believing and understanding. Your wisdom and theirs come from the same Spirit.

- You **pray together**, thanking God for blessings, reaching for strength, asking for guidance in crisis and doubt. You know as you gather—restless toddlers, searching teenagers, harried adults—that God answers all prayers, but sometimes in surprising ways.

- You **serve one another**, often sacrificing your own wants, for the other's good. You struggle to take up your cross and carry it with love. Your "deaths" and "risings" become compelling signs of Jesus' own life, death, and resurrection.

- You **forgive and seek reconciliation**. Over and over, you let go of old hurts and grudges to make peace with one another. And family members come to believe that, no matter what, they are still loved by you and by God.

- You **celebrate** life—birthdays and weddings, births and deaths, a first day of school and a graduation, rites of passage into adulthood, new jobs, old friends, family reunions, surprise visits, holy days and holidays. You come together when tragedy strikes and in joyful celebration of the sacraments. As you gather for a meal, you break bread and share stories, becoming more fully the community of love Jesus calls us to be.

- You **welcome** the stranger, the lonely one, the grieving person into your home. You give drink to the thirsty and food to the hungry. The Gospel assures us that when we do this, they are strangers no more, but Christ.

- You **act justly** in your community when you treat others with respect, stand against discrimination and racism, and work to overcome hunger, poverty, homelessness, illiteracy.

- You **affirm life** as a precious gift from God. You oppose whatever destroys life, such as abortion, euthanasia, unjust war, capital punishment, neighborhood and domestic violence, poverty and racism. Within your family, when you shun violent words and actions and look for peaceful ways to resolve conflict, you become a voice for life, forming peacemakers for the next generation.

- You **raise up vocations** to the priesthood and religious life as you encourage your children to listen for God's call and respond to God's grace. This is especially fostered through family prayer, involvement in parish life, and by the way you speak of priests, sisters, brothers, and permanent deacons.

No domestic church does all this perfectly. But neither does any parish or diocesan church. All members of the Church struggle daily to become more faithful disciples of Christ.

We need to enable families to recognize that they are a domestic church. There may be families who do not understand or believe they are a domestic church. Maybe they feel overwhelmed by this calling or unable to carry out its responsibilities. Perhaps they consider their family too "broken" to be used for the Lord's purposes. But remember, a family is holy not because it is perfect but because God's grace is at work in it, helping it to set out anew every day on the way of love.

Like the whole Church, every Christian family rests on a firm foundation, namely, Christ's promise to be faithful to those he has chosen. When a man and a woman pledge themselves to each other in the sacrament of matrimony, they join in Christ's promise and become a living sign of his union with the Church (cf. Eph 5:32).

Therefore, a committed, permanent, faithful relationship of husband and wife is the root of a family. It strengthens all the members, provides best for the needs of children, and causes the church of the home to be an effective sign of Christ in the world.

Wherever a family exists and love still moves through its members, grace is present. Nothing—not even divorce or death— can place limits upon God's gracious love.

And so, we recognize the courage and determination of families with one parent raising the children. Somehow you fulfill your call to create a good home, care for your children, hold down a job, and undertake responsibilities in the neighborhood and church. You reflect the power of faith, the strength of love, and the certainty that God does not abandon us when circumstances leave you alone in parenting.

Those who try to blend two sets of children into one family face a special challenge to accept differences and to love unconditionally. They offer us a practical example of peacemaking.

Families arising from an interreligious marriage give witness to the universality of God's love which overcomes all division. When family members respect one another's different religious beliefs and practices, they testify to our deeper unity as a human family called to live in peace with one another. We share the pain of couples who struggle without success to conceive a child. We admire and encourage families who adopt a child, become foster parents, or care for an elderly or disabled relative in their homes.

We offer our heartfelt sympathy and support to those parents who grieve at the death of a child due to illness, stillbirth, or the violence so prevalent in our society today.

We honor all families who, in the face of obstacles, remain faithful to Christ's way of love. The church of the home can live and grow in every family.

In our pastoral ministry, we have listened to many families: to husbands and wives, to estranged spouses, to abused and abandoned spouses, to single parents, and to children. We know that all families long for the peace, the acceptance, a sense of purpose, and the reconciliation that the term **church of the home** suggests. We believe that with prayer; hard work; understanding; commitment; the support of other families, parish priests, deacons and their wives, and religious and lay pastoral ministers; and especially with God's grace, the church of the home is built in ordinary homes, in your family.

Reflection Questions

1. Reflect for a moment on your life as a family. Do you recall a time when you felt God's presence in your midst?
2. Why do you think this was so?
3. What was happening?
4. Recall one or more instances where you experienced being **church**, either in the home or outside of it. What was the outcome?

Recall how the wayward son
swallowed his pride and
returned home to find a
forgiving father awaiting him
and a family celebrating his
arrival (cf. Lk 15:11-32).
In the same way, all of us
who suffer broken relationships are called to make
peace, to reestablish trust,
and to repledge love.

Families Are Challenged by Change and Complexity

LIVING IN TODAY'S SOCIETY

We know you face obstacles as you try to maintain strong family ties and to follow your calling as a church of the home. The rapid pace of social change; the religious, ethnic, and cultural diversity of our society; the revolution of values within our culture; the intrusion of mass media; the impact of political and economic conditions: all these place families under considerable stress.

Some family pressures are due to broad social forces over which a family has little control. But other pressures are caused by personal choices, sometimes involving human weakness and sinful behavior.

Divorce, a serious contemporary problem, takes a heavy toll on family life. Spouses and children are affected most immediately, but so too are grandparents, other relatives, and friends that make up the extended family.

Divorce can create in young people a fear of and a reluctance to make life-long commitments. It often pushes families into poverty and contributes to other social ills.

Families are burdened also by the economic demands of providing housing, health care, childcare when needed, education, and proper care for sick or elderly members. Unemployment or the fear of losing a job haunts many families.

Child and spouse abuse are touching the lives of more families. So, too, is the tragedy of AIDS. Families struggle with alcoholism, crime and gang violence in their neighborhoods, substance abuse, and suicide among youth. In a never-ending stream, communications media bring images and messages into your homes that may contradict your values and exert a negative influence on your children.

Some families face multiple burdens of poverty, racism, religious and cultural discrimination. New immigrant families can feel unwelcome in our communities and caught in a conflict between cultures.

Not all families experience these pressures to the same degree. Some are damaged by forces beyond their control. Many more, however, continue with prayerful determination and trust in God. All deserve our compassion and support—those who persevere also our gratitude as they show us the very faithfulness of God.

Pressure is brought to bear on families not only by outside forces but by those ordinary and inevitable tensions which arise from within. Daily you discover how different temperaments and opposing points of view can create hard feelings and even lasting bitterness. Human weakness and sinfulness often make it difficult to accept differences.

Recall how the wayward son swallowed his pride and returned home to find a forgiving father awaiting him and a family celebrating his arrival (cf. Lk 15:11-32). In the same way, all of us who suffer broken relationships are called to make peace, to reestablish trust, and to repledge love.

This can be an especially painful task for parents. What if your child becomes addicted to drugs, or harms others through drunken driving, or chooses friends you consider a bad influence? What if your adult child leaves the Church or makes other choices that cause you pain? Is it still possible to maintain a loving relationship  without approving the child's behavior? How much can you accept before you compromise your own integrity?

It's not possible in this message to give complete answers to these questions and to the many others you confront. But what we can do, as your pastors and teachers, is to shed the light of Sacred Scripture and our Catholic tradition on a few key issues which you face.

In the next few pages we would like to discuss with you four challenges in family life. They are: living faithfully, giving life, growing in mutuality, and taking time. They make a claim on your resources and responsibilities as a church of the home. They point out how you can *follow the way of love, even as Christ loved you* (cf. Eph 5:2).

Reflection Questions

1. Can you think of a pressure that has brought trouble to your family?
2. How did you deal with it?
3. Did this bring you closer or drive you farther apart as a family?

LIVING FAITHFULLY
The Sacred Scripture passage that many couples choose for their wedding ceremony is a marvelous blueprint for loving.

Love is patient, love is kind. It is not jealous, [love] is not pompous, it is not inflated, it is not rude, it does not seek its own interests, it is not quick-tempered, it does not brood over injury, it does not rejoice over wrongdoing, but rejoices with the truth. It bears all things, believes all things, hopes all things, endures all things. Love never fails. (1 Cor 13:4-8)

These words of St. Paul are worth daily meditation not only for their insight into the true shape of love but for strengthening our wills to follow this way of love. The love that he describes flourishes in faithful, stable relationships. This applies, first and foremost, to a marriage. It is true also for the entire family.

When a woman and a man vow to be true in good times and in bad they are confirming a decision to love one another. But, as married couples have taught us, this decision to love is one we have to make over and over again, when it feels good and when it does not. It is a decision to look for, act on, and pray for the good of the people we say we love. It is a pledge of fidelity.

Our world today needs living witnesses to fidelity. These are the most convincing signs of the love that Christ has for every human being. Couples who are living faithful lives of mutual love and support—though not without difficulties—have the gratitude of the whole Church.

You know the value of a loving and life-giving marriage. Indeed, your marriage is a gift to all of us. A wonderful way to share this gift, as well as to

reinvigorate your own commitment, would be to help engaged couples pre-
pare for the sacrament of matrimony. We invite you to become part of this
important ministry through a parish or diocesan program.

Couples who are finding it hard to stay married deserve our prayers and
assistance. The Church can offer them the counsel of other married couples
and the assurance that, with God's grace, it is possible to live their vocation.

Newly married couples, when you find yourselves in a crisis, do not con-
clude that divorce is inevitable. All of us—family members, friends, communities of faith—should feel responsible for helping you to recognize that
divorce is not inevitable and is certainly not your only option.

An enduring marriage is more than simply endurance. It is a process of
growth into an intimate friendship and a deepening peace. So we urge all
couples: renew your commitment regularly, seek enrichment often, and ask
for pastoral and professional help when needed.

To live faithfully in a marriage requires humility, trust, compromise, communication, and a sense of humor. It is a give-and-take experience, involving hurt and forgiveness, failure and sacrifice. The very same thing is true
of fidelity in other family relationships.

Children who care for
parents stricken with
Alzheimer's disease, par-
ents who stand by their
adult children even when
they seem to reject the
family's values, a grand-
parent who helps to raise
the children when parents
are unable, a single parent
who goes to great lengths
to raise and nurture the children without the benefit of the other parent: all
these are living faithful lives. They enflesh the words of Ruth, who refused to

forsake her widowed mother-in-law, Naomi, and instead vowed, "wherever you go I will go" (Ru 1:16).

Your faithful love in a marriage and family is tested by change. It can also be strengthened and brought to maturity through change. The challenge is to remain open to the Lord's gracious, healing presence and to see change as an opportunity for growth.

Some changes in a family come unexpectedly, like a major illness, a job transfer, or loss of employment. Others fit more naturally into the flow of life, such as the birth of a child, the arrival of teenage years, or adult children leaving home. Regardless, though, every change brings with it a measure of stress and uncertainty. For many, it is like a dark night of the soul.

In these moments, dare to hope that you will rise to new experiences of love, entering into the very mystery of Christ's own dying and rising.

Maybe your family is trying to cope with a difficult loss or change. Perhaps you are torn by a conflict or trapped in an unhealthy pattern of relationships. If this is so, please seek God's help and the support of the Church.

The Church's treasures of prayer and worship, learning and service, contemplation and spiritual guidance are always available to you. The grace of the sacrament of matrimony and the power of the commitment that you have made to one another are continuing wellsprings of strength.

A marriage between a Christian and a follower of another religion, while not a sacrament, is a holy state instituted by God. It too is a divine gift with sustaining spiritual power.

Also, do not hesitate to seek professional assistance. Counseling, for example, can help you to identify the personal resources you already have and to use them more effectively.

1. What does *love* mean to you?
2. When have you had to renew a decision to love your spouse, child, or another family member?
3. What made it difficult or easy?

GIVING LIFE

St. Thomas Aquinas taught that love diffuses itself, that is, it wells up and spills over into every aspect of our lives.

When a man and a woman marry they pledge a love which is, in the words of Pope Paul VI, *creative of life* (cf. *On Human Life*, no. 9). For a "couple, while giving themselves to one another, give not just themselves but also

the reality of their children, who are a living reflection of their love . . ." (*On the Family*, no. 14).

Welcoming a child, through birth or adoption, is an act of faith as well as an act of love. Being open to new life signals trust in the God who ultimately creates and sustains all life. It is also the beginning of a lifetime commandment: nurturing, teaching, disciplining, and, finally, letting go of a child—as he or she follows a new and perhaps uncharted way of love. Parenthood is indeed a Christian call and responsibility. It is the experience of acting as God's instruments in giving life to sons and daughters in various ways; but equally, it is an experience of being formed by God through your children.

The life that you give as parents is not restricted just to your offspring. The children of other families need your guidance, as do other parents who can benefit from your hard-earned experience. Likewise, you cannot raise your own children alone. All families—even those with two parents—need a wider circle of aunts and uncles, grandparents, godparents, and other faith-filled families.

There are so many ways in which families can give life, especially in a society that devalues life through such actions as abortion and euthanasia. For instance, your family can ask: how have we been blessed as a family? What values and beliefs do we want to hand on to future generations? What strengths and resources do we possess that we could share with others? What traditions and rituals have enriched our lives? Could they benefit other families?

Each generation of a family is challenged to leave the world a more beautiful and beneficial place than it inherited. You can do this, for example, when you deliberately pass on your wisdom and the faith of the Church, providing countercultural messages about poverty, consumerism, sexuality and racial justice—to name a few.

You also give life as a family by doing such simple things as taking a grandparent out of a nursing home for a ride, bringing a meal to a sick neighbor, helping to build homes for poor people, working in a soup kitchen, recycling your goods, working to improve the schools, or joining political action on behalf of those treated unjustly.

Such activity builds stronger family bonds. It enriches both the receiver and the giver. It releases the "formidable energies" present in families for building a better society (*On the Family*, no. 43). The value of your witness which Christian families offer cannot be overestimated. As a family becomes a community of faith and love, it simultaneously becomes a center of evangelization.

Reflection Questions

1. What is it in life that matters most to me?
2. How, with whom—and when—shall I share my treasure?
3. Does our family share what it treasures with other families?

GROWING IN MUTUALITY

At the basis of all relationships in a family is our fundamental equality as persons created in God's image. The creation narratives in the Book of Genesis teach this fundamental truth: "both man and woman are human beings to an equal degree, both are created in God's image" (*On the Dignity and Vocation of Women*, no. 6).

And St. Paul describes the "new creation" made possible in Christ:

> For all of you who were baptized into Christ have clothed yourselves with Christ. There is neither Jew nor Greek, there is neither slave nor free person, there is not male and female; for you are all one in Christ Jesus. (Gal 3:27-28)

Marriage is the partnership of a man and woman equal in dignity and value. This does not imply sameness in roles or expectations. There are important physical and psychological traits which result in differing skills and perspectives. Nor does the equality of persons mean that two spouses will have identical gifts or character or roles.

Rather, a couple who accepts their equality as sons and daughters in the Lord will honor and cherish one another. They will respect and value each other's gifts and uniqueness. They will "[b]e subordinate to one another out of reverence for Christ" (Eph 5:21).

Our competitive culture tends to promote aggressiveness and struggles for power. These are a common part of life, especially in the workplace. It is all too easy for couples to bring an unhealthy competitive spirit to their relationship. The Gospel demands that all of us critically examine such attitudes. Marriage must never become a struggle for control.

For, unlike other relationships, marriage is a vowed covenant with unique dimensions. In. this partnership, mutual submission—not dominance by either partner—is the key to genuine joy. Our attitude should be the same as Jesus "[w]ho, though he was in the form of God, did not regard equality with God something to be grasped. Rather, he emptied himself . . ." (Phil 2:6-7).

True equality, understood as mutuality, is not measuring out tasks (who prepares the meals, who supervises homework, and so forth) or maintaining an orderly schedule. It thrives at a much deeper level where the power of the Spirit resides. Here, the grace of the vowed life not only makes the shedding of willfulness possible, but also leads to a joyful willingness.

Mutuality is really about sharing power and exercising responsibility for a purpose larger than ourselves. How household duties are distributed should follow from understanding what it takes to build a life together, as well as the individual skills and interests you bring to your common life.

Our experience as pastors shows us that genuine marital intimacy and true friendship are unlikely without mutuality. One spouse alone is not the keeper of love's flame. Both of you are co-creators of your relationship. Nowhere is this more vividly portrayed than in your decisions about having children. The Church promotes natural family planning for many reasons, among which are that "it favors attention for one's partner, helps both parties to drive out selfishness, the enemy of true love, and deepens their sense of responsibility" (*On Human Life*, no. 21).

Agreeing that you are equal might be easier than changing your behavior or accepting joint responsibility for your relationship. It takes hard work to really understand another's feelings or to practice shared decision making on important matters.

Sharing feelings and a willingness to be vulnerable can be difficult, particularly for those of us raised in the "strong and silent" tradition. Men in all walks of life seem to have been influenced by this unwritten norm.

Moreover, some women have learned to fear conflict and may remain passive in the face of it. Women who accept their own self-worth are more able to express their beliefs, ideas, and feelings, even such painful ones as anger.

Flexible roles may appear difficult if your families of origin did not model them. Each family (couple) must decide what is best for them in a spirit of respect and mutuality. Especially when both spouses are employed, household duties need to be shared.

We urge you to take advantage of programs sponsored by your parish, diocese, or other organizations in your community that teach communication and conflict resolution to couples and to parents. Also there are worthwhile programs that lead women and men to a spiritual understanding of their behaviors, to appreciate how they influence each other, and to move beyond gender stereotypes.

We urge you to join with other couples and families who are making a conscious effort to follow Christ's way of love. You can find help for this through the Christian Family Movement (CFM), Marriage Encounter, Teams of Our Lady, the New Families Movement, and your diocesan Family Life Office—to name just a few.

When children are born, both mother and father are important in nurturing and forming them. More and more, fathers have been discovering how their involvement in parenting enriches both their children and themselves. This is a hopeful development.

We urge men to interpret their traditional role as "provider" for a family in more than an economic sense. Physical care of children, discipline, training in religious values and practices, helping with school work and other activities: all these and more can be provided by fathers as well as mothers.

There is a lesson to be learned from the way in which many cultures place children at the center of family life. Children in the family share equal dignity as persons with the adults. They too are part of the covenant of mutuality. Parents can demonstrate this by treating children with respect, giving them responsibilities, listening seriously to their thoughts and feelings.

Bringing children into decision-making discussions, especially when the decisions could alter the pattern of family life, has precedent in our tradition. We read in the Rule of St. Benedict that the abbot is to consult with all members of the monastery, even the youngest (who often were children), when their lives were likely to be affected. Rather than undermining authority, this strengthens it in love.

Elders enrich the life of their families. They, too, should be cherished, not merely tolerated, for they are "a witness to the past and a source of wisdom for the young and for the future" (*On the Family*, no. 27). Grandparents, we encourage you to continue your lives of caring, especially for the youngest generation, and to find additional ways of demonstrating love for your children and grandchildren.

The pattern of mutuality within a household is closely allied with the virtue of humility. And humility is forged in prayer: husbands and wives praying with and for each other, parents praying with and for their children. This is the heart of ministry within the church of the home.

Reflection Questions

1. As a married couple, reread this section and consider: how has early life shaped our understanding of the roles of men and women?
2. Where do we need to grow in mutuality?
3. As a family, do we show respect for one another?
4. How can we strengthen this virtue?

TAKING TIME

We are struck by the incredible busyness of family life that can take its toll on loving relationships. Daily we observe families overwhelmed by the demands of work, business travel, household tasks, getting to and from school, keeping appointments with doctors, civic responsibilities, and volunteering.

Both men and women can get caught up in long hours and weekends at their place of work. Balancing home and work responsibilities is a shared obligation for spouses. It is a critical issue facing families today. Where choices exist, hours on the job need to be weighed against their impact on family life.

To thrive, love requires attention, communication, and time—to share a story or confide a need, to play a game, to tell a joke, to watch and cheer on—time to be present to another's failure or success, confusion, despair or moment of decision.

Spending time together builds intimacy, increases understanding and creates memories between husband and wife, parent and child, brothers and sisters, grandparents and younger family members. It is hard to imagine how a family can live faithfully, be life giving, and grow in mutuality without deliberately choosing to spend time together.

It is especially important for couples to have some time alone. Spending time away from children and other adults provides opportunities to grow in understanding and rekindles the fire of love that is often left unattended as children, job, and other commitments claim time and energy.

So, each of us needs to ask: to what am I giving my precious time? What are my priorities? Do television, sports, making money, shopping, getting ahead on the job, volunteering in the church or community swallow up time that could be better spent with those I love?

We challenge you to examine the priorities you have for your family. Compare them with how you actually spend your time. See what individual pursuits could be given up or replaced with family activities. We urge you to take time to be together:

• Making shared meals a priority (even if you gather at a fast food restaurant),
• Praying and worshipping together, especially at the Sunday Eucharist and in family prayers, such as the rosary,
• Building family traditions and rituals,
• Taking part in retreats and family education programs.

Watching television together and discussing the values being promoted on programs can be time well spent as a family.

Time given to solitude is also time well spent. When we enter into a genuine Sabbath experience, alone with God, we can understand more fully who we are—as distinguished from what we do—and can receive what Jesus offers when he invites us to "come to me . . . and I will refresh you" (Mt 11:28).

Reflection Questions

1. How are we balancing time commitments to jobs, community, each other, and the children?
2. Have our lives become too fragmented?
3. What positive choices have we made, this week, to improve on how we use our time?

Families Are Supported in the Church

AN INVITATION

Earlier in our message we affirmed the ancient insight that the Christian family is a church of the home. This understanding has guided and informed all we have written. We know that, in the everyday moments of your family lives, you proclaim God's word, communicate with God in prayer, and serve the needs of others. The graced experience you have as a Christian family in your domestic church should be shared more extensively with all of us.

We encourage you to help the Church by speaking to us, but more importantly to other families, about how you are trying to follow the way of love. Tell us how you work to stay married, how your family has overcome obstacles, how you have made time for each other, sought enrichment opportunities or professional help with your problems. Share with us how you have come to understand your vocation as a spouse or parent. Speak to us of

your pain over broken promises and relationships. Give witness to your belief in God's mercy as you move toward reconciliation both with your family and with the Church. Help us to appreciate the symbols and traditions with which you celebrate and worship. Let us glimpse how you are trying to live a more simple lifestyle, serve the needy, build justice and peace in your community. Tell us what kinds of support you expect from the larger Church.

In 1994 (The International Year of the Family) Catholic News Service will provide a forum, through its syndicated "Faith Alive" series, for families to tell their stories.

Your words and deeds will lend strength to our exhortations.

OUR PLEDGE

At other times we have urged all institutions of society to forge partnerships with families. We now promise to do our part to develop such a partnership within the Church. Specifically, as the U.S. Conference of Catholic Bishops, we pledge:

- To welcome dialogue between our conference and families by asking the Committee on Marriage and Family to find ways of listening to families' reflections on this message;

- To continue our support for families organizing to help one another, e.g., in the responsibilities of parenthood, in the process of grieving and healing after a significant loss, in taking action to serve the poor and remedy injustice, in forming communities of families who walk the way of love together;

- To request theologians and pastoral leaders, especially at the national level, to develop resources that will strengthen the unity of marriage and deepen everyone's understanding of the value and role of the Christian family as a domestic church;

- To study in greater depth how to improve our marriage preparation efforts and how to strengthen and enrich marriages, using the spiritual and pastoral resources of the Church, and to focus particularly on those stages in a marriage when there is the greatest likelihood of divorce;

- To include more deliberately within the scope of our pastoral care an attentiveness to single-parent families, families in a second marriage, grandparents raising children, interracial families, interfaith families, and persons who are widowed or divorced;

- To broaden our efforts to welcome families from ethnically and racially-diverse groups;

- To advocate with national organizations, publishers, educators, and other experts for resources that will assist parents in the role of forming the morals and faith of their children;

- To continue our national advocacy for public policy and legislation that will promote family stability and the welfare of children and those who are most vulnerable—the unborn, the disabled, and the frail and sick elderly.

In general, we wish to initiate or improve things that are within our competence as a national body so that our belief about you, a church of the home, will bear fruit. We bishops need you to infuse the whole Church with your vitality, your understanding, your loving intimacy, your hospitality. We need you, whose faith and discipleship are nurtured within the church of the home, to join more fully with us in proclaiming Christ to the world.

SOME CHALLENGES

We acknowledge that official structures sometimes make it difficult to have dialogue with families and to create a partnership with you. Therefore, as bishops in our individual dioceses, we recognize these challenges:

- To urge our diocesan agencies and parishes to create ways for families to communicate with church leadership about their needs and their strengths;

- To see that our parishes, schools, institutions, and diocesan agencies examine the extent to which their policies and programs help or hinder family growth and enable families to meet their responsibilities;

- To give serious consideration to changing those policies and programs that are no longer responsive to contemporary family needs or make it difficult for families to assume their rightful place as a church of the home.

A CONCLUDING WORD

We have expressed in various ways throughout our message how deeply we care about strengthening family life for the well-being of the world and the Church and, indeed, for the sake of every man, woman, and child. Now, as a means of emphasizing, we offer these reflections:

- *Married couples*: the grace of the sacrament of matrimony and the spiritual power of your vows are available to you daily. Call upon these realities to strengthen you in your vocation.

- *Parents*: not only do your children need discipline and love, they need the example of adults whose behavior demonstrates their caring. Put your children first in making decisions about family life.

- *Children and youth*: you have the right to expect love, guidance, discipline, and respect from your parents and elders. And, in turn, you should obey and respect them while you share with them your love, your experience of God, your fears and hope. You should help your parents and elders in their needs and accompany them in the way of holiness. Pray for them as they do for you.

- *Spouses who are separated*: the road to healing, reconciliation, and rebuilding of your relationship can be a slow, painful one. If you are willing to begin that journey, the Church has many resources like pastoral counseling, Retrouvaille, and The Third Option program, which can assist you.

- *Divorced and widowed persons*: relationships and circumstances within your family may have changed, but God's love for you is ever present and does not come to an end. Grasp the hands of those who reach out to you in loving concern. Extend your own hand to others whom you meet on the road to healing and reconciliation. There is a home for you within our parishes and communities of faith.

- *Single parents*: to be faced with all the responsibilities of parenting by yourself is a challenge that touches the very core of your life. We bishops express our solidarity with you. We urge all parishes and Christian communities to welcome you, to help you find what you need for a good family life, and to offer the loving friendship that is a mark of our Christian tradition.

- *Families*: join with other families in communities of mutual support. Spiritual growth, insight into problems, help in times of trouble, and lasting friendships can flow from such experiences.

- There is no shame in seeking help for family problems, whether it be in the form of counseling, educational programs, or support groups.

- Christian life includes obligations beyond the family circle. For children to learn the true meaning of abundant life in Christ (cf. Jn 10:10), they need to know the joy of contributing to the common good: in the home, in the neighborhood, in the Church, and in society. Duty is an anchor in what seems an ocean of chaos.

If all the members of the Church are to follow Christ's way of love, it is essential that we continue speaking with, listening to, and learning from each other. We are the one Body of Christ: the Church in the home, in the small community, in the parish, in the diocese, in a universal communion. We share one Lord, one faith, one baptism. We are one family in Christ!

We bishops prayerfully entrust all families
to Mary, the mother of Jesus
and mother of the Church.
We ask St. Joseph to guide you
in all the ways of faithfulness.

Appendix

TEACHING AND PASTORAL DOCUMENTS ON MARRIAGE AND FAMILY LIFE

Most of these documents (those listed with a publication number) are available from USCCB Publishing, 3211 Fourth Street NE, Washington, D.C. 20017. 800-235-8722.

Second Vatican Council. *Constitution on the Church in the Modern World/Gaudium et Spes.* December 7, 1965. (Not currently available from USCCB; please check with your parish or diocesan library.)

Teaching on the dignity of marriage, the role of the family, and the duty of society and the Church to support families.

Pope Paul VI. *On Human Life/Humanae Vitae* (also known as *On the Regulation of Birth*). July 25, 1968. Publication No. 280-2.

Encyclical letter on the nature and purposes of married love, the gift of fertility, and the call to responsible parenthood.

Pope John Paul II. *On the Family/Familiaris Consortio.* December 15, 1981. Publication No. 833-9.

Apostolic exhortation on the nature and tasks of the Christian family and the scope of pastoral care needed by families.

Pope John Paul II. *On the Dignity and Vocation of Women/Mulieris Dignitatem.* August 15, 1988. (Not currently available from USCCB; please check with your parish or diocesan library.)

The mutuality of men and women in marriage, the importance of the order of love, and the essential Marian dimension of the Church are presented in this apostolic letter which springs from the Holy Father's meditation on the Scriptures.

National Conference of Catholic Bishops. *Human Life in Our Day*. November 15, 1968. (Not currently available from USCCB; please check with your parish or diocesan library.)

Pastoral letter emphasizing the maturing of life in a family and the development of life in a peaceful world order.

National Conference of Catholic Bishops. *To Live in Christ Jesus: A Pastoral Reflection on the Moral Life*. November 11, 1976. (Not currently available from USCCB; please check with your parish or diocesan library.)

Pastoral letter responding to certain moral questions arising from life in the family, nation, and world community.

Holy See. *Charter of the Rights of the Family*. October 22, 1983. (Not currently available from USCCB; please check with your parish or diocesan library.)

A document addressed to governments presenting principles to be used in drawing up legislation, family policy and programs.

Pontifical Council for Promoting Christian Unity. *Directory for the Application of Principles and Norms on Ecumenism*. March 25, 1993. Publication No. 658-1.

A document containing important directives on mixed marriages.

National Conference of Catholic Bishops. *Family Ministry: A Pastoral Plan and a Reaffirmation*. November 13, 1990. Publication No. 426-0.

Statement providing leadership and direction for pastoral ministry with families.

United States Catholic Conference. *Human Sexuality: A Catholic Perspective for Education and Lifelong Learning*. November 21, 1990. Publication No. 405-8.

Document presenting the human values, scriptural roots, moral principles, and theological considerations that must be taken into account when formulating educational programs.

United States Catholic Conference. *Putting Children and Families First: A Challenge for Our Church, Nation, and World*. November 1991. Publication No. 469-4.

Pastoral statement examining the social conditions of children and the moral and religious dimensions of caring for them, especially through reordering our priorities in public policy and legislation.

Committee on Marriage and Family, NCCB. *A Family Perspective in Church and Society: 10th Anniversary Edition*. 1998. Publication No. 5-273.

A resource for leaders to increase their understanding of contemporary families and to assess how policies and programs can strengthen family life.

Committee for Pastoral Research and Practices, NCCB. *Faithful to Each Other Forever: A Catholic Handbook of Pastoral Help for Marriage Preparation*. 1989. Publication No. 252-7.

A resource for diocesan and parish ministers responsible for catechesis on the sacrament of matrimony, preparing couples for marriage, and providing pastoral care after the wedding.

Committee on Marriage and Family, NCCB. *Families at the Center: A Handbook for Parish Ministry with a Family Perspective*. 1990. Publication No. 337-X.

A resource for those who want to know how the principles of a family perspective can be utilized in parish ministries.

Committee on Marriage and Family and Committee on Women in Society and in the Church, NCCB. *When I Call for Help: A Pastoral Response to Domestic Violence against Women*. 1992. Publication No. 547-X.

A statement intended for the victims of abuse, for those to whom they turn for help, and for abusers themselves; it offers moral and practical guidance for responding to domestic violence and for dealing with those who abuse women.

Committee for Pro-Life Activities, NCCB. *Human Sexuality from God's Perspective: Humanae Vitae 25 Years Later.* July 25, 1993. (Available from: Diocesan Development Program for Natural Family Planning, 3211 Fourth Street NE, Washington, D.C. 20017. 202-541-3070.)

A reaffirmation of the teaching of *Humanae Vitae* calling a new generation to recognize and accept the Church's prophetic vision of marriage, sexuality, and family life.